YOUR SENSATIONAL SENSE OF SMELL

BY JULIA VOGEL • ILLUSTRATED BY ROBERT SQUIER

The Child's World

Published by The Child's World®
1980 Lookout Drive • Mankato, MN 56003-1705
800-599-READ • www.childsworld.com

ACKNOWLEDGMENTS
The Child's World®: Mary Berendes, Publishing Director
The Design Lab: Design and production
Red Line Editorial: Editorial direction

LIBRARY OF CONGRESS CATALOGING-IN-PUBLICATION DATA
Vogel, Julia.
  Your sensational sense of smell / by Julia Vogel;
illustrated by Robert Squier.
    p. cm.
  Includes bibliographical references and index.
  ISBN 978-1-60954-288-7 (library bound : alk. paper)
  1. Smell—Juvenile literature. 2. Nose—Juvenile literature. I. Squier,
Robert, ill. II. Title.
  QP458.V64 2011
  612.8'6—dc22   2010037847

Printed in the United States of America
Mankato, MN
December, 2010
PA02068

ABOUT THE AUTHOR

Julia Vogel has a nose for the latest science news. An award-winning author, she has a bachelor's degree in biology and a doctorate in forestry. Julia's all-time favorite smells are pine trees, campfires, and just-washed baby hair.

ABOUT THE ILLUSTRATOR

Robert Squier has been drawing ever since he could hold a crayon. Today, instead of using crayons, he uses pencils, paint, and the computer. Robert lives in New Hampshire with his wife, Jessica, and a dog named "Q."

HI! My name is Daisy. I smell wonderful on a warm spring day. There are lots of other smells to enjoy, too. Fresh-cut grass has a great scent! How about big piles of fall leaves?

Your sense of smell tells you things about your surroundings. But what is a sense? And how does smell work? Join me on a scent safari to explore this sensational sense. Let's hit the trail!

SNIFF! SNIFF! Burgers are grilling in the park. The picnic table is set with colorful plates.

RUFF! RUFF! A dog barks at a furry, black-and-white visitor.

P-YEW! Everyone runs away.

These sights, sounds, and smells tell you what happened. A skunk cancelled the party!

Seeing, hearing, and smelling are senses. Tasting and touching are, too. These five senses help you understand the world around you. Let's sniff out more about them.

Your senses gather information you need to be happy and healthy.

AAAH. Fresh air blows through an open window.

MMMM! Grandma is frying banana pancakes.

Body parts for each sense collect information. Then they send messages to your brain. Your eyes, ears, tongue, and skin are all **sense organs**. But my favorite sense organ is the one you can follow to fresh-baked bread or lilac blooms. It's your nifty, sniffy nose!

6

Smelling starts with breathing. Close your mouth and take a deep breath. Air flows into your nose through two nostrils. A sticky liquid called **mucus** lines each nostril. Mucus traps dust and **germs** from the air so they won't reach your lungs.

Scent chemicals also flow in when you breathe. These are tiny bits of **odors**. The air rushes down to your lungs. But scent chemicals stick at the top of the **nasal cavity**.

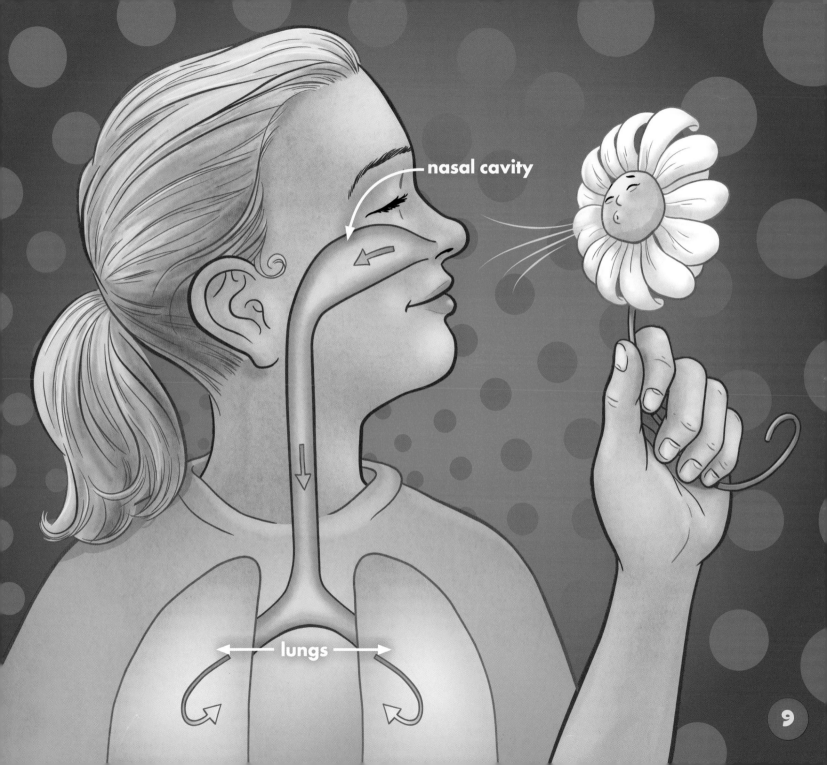

nasal cavity

lungs

Inside your nasal cavity are two patches of skin about the size of your big toenails. Each mucus-covered patch is packed with tiny smell **sensors**. These grab on to the odors you smell.

You have about 100 million smell sensors in your nose. Seems smelly, huh? With so many sensors, smell is a super-sensitive sense. People can figure out 10,000 odors. Isn't that amazing?

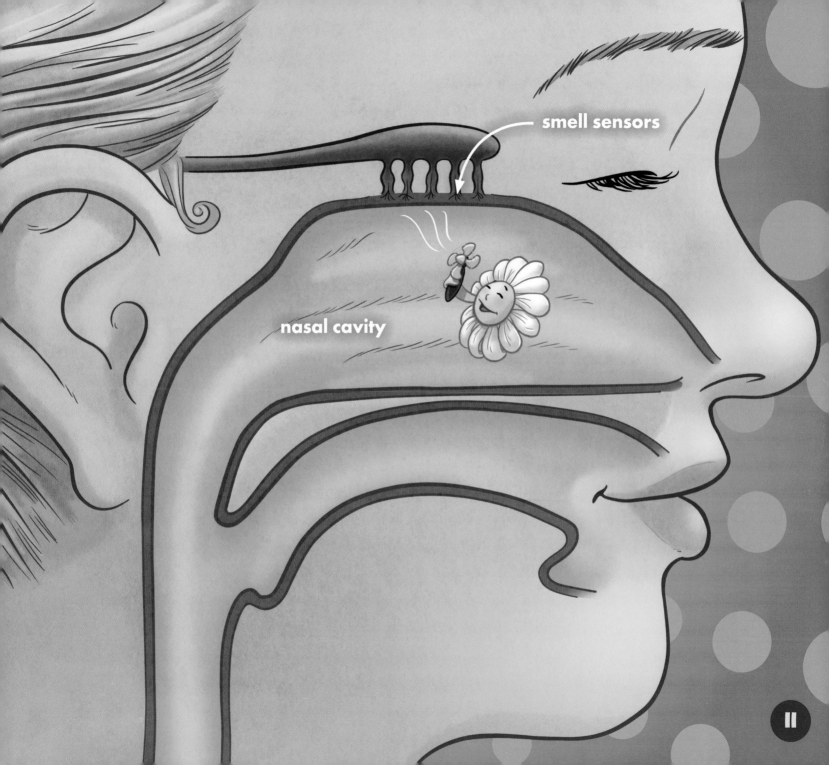

At the bottom of each smell sensor are tiny hair-like cells. They poke into the nasal cavity and catch scent chemicals in the mucus.

Like puzzle pieces, each odor only fits with one kind of sensor. That means a rose's sweet scent can't be picked up by the sensors for sweaty feet.

The tops of the sensors pass through small holes in your skull bone. Then they connect with the **olfactory bulb**.

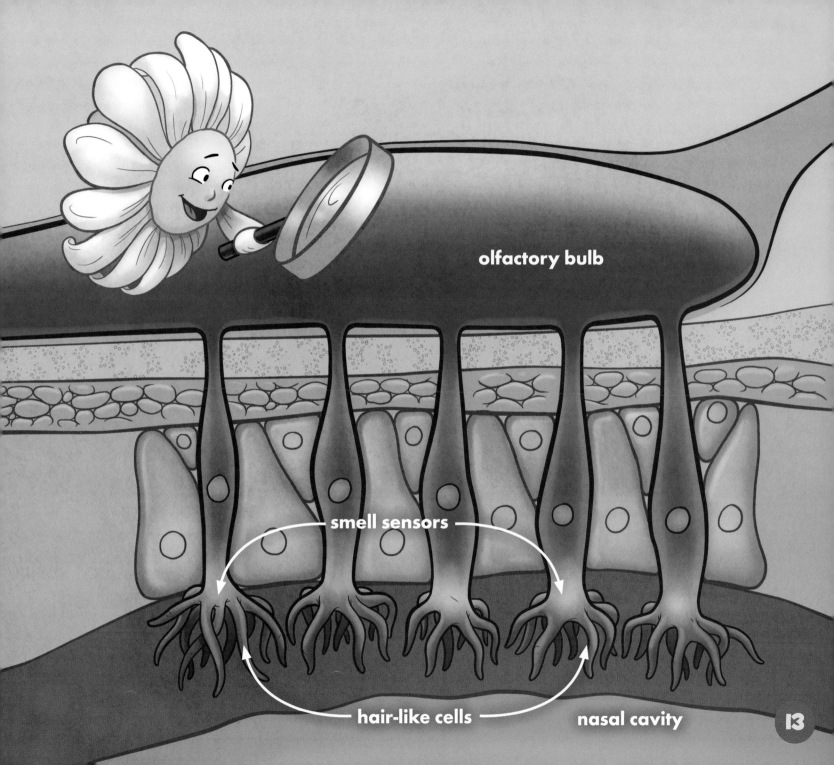

olfactory bulb

smell sensors

hair-like cells

nasal cavity

13

The olfactory bulb is a part of your brain. This brain part receives messages from your smell sensors. Traveling along **nerves**, or pathways, the messages go to other parts of the brain. The brain then figures out what you smell. Take a sniff of your sandwich. Smells like peanut butter and jelly!

So, it's really your brain that understands smells, not your nose. How cool!

Smells don't only come from the air you breathe in through your nose. Some smells come from inside your mouth. Smell chemicals from food break off in your mouth when you chew. When you breathe out through your nose, they flow from your mouth up to your nasal cavity. The smell sensors are there to catch them.

And that's a good thing. Smell and taste are linked to each other. Without smell, food wouldn't be so delicious. Test this the next time you have a stuffy nose. Can you taste the chicken in your soup—or does it taste like nothing?

Let's move on to see how smells shape your life. Some people think it's not as important as sight or touch. Smelling is even called the forgotten sense.

But smelling is helpful. Newborn babies find their mother's milk by scent. New moms know their babies by smell, too.

Each of us has our own special scent. It comes from many things—from the soap you use to your mood. Does your mom smell different if she's happy or mad?

Smelling also keeps you safe. The smell of smoke warns you there's a fire. A sour smell tells you milk has gone bad and keeps you from drinking it. Bad smells sometimes come from germs that could make you sick. So, a stinky smell means stay away. And, body odor tells you to take a bath!

You enjoy many odors, like the fruity scent of your shampoo and bubble bath. How about the warm earth after a spring rain? Good smells make our lives happier and more fun.

PEE-YEW!

Smells even help us remember happy and sad times in the past. That's because smell messages go to the part of the brain that stores memories. It's called the **hippocampus**.

The scent of pine trees makes you think of your favorite camping trip in the woods.

A whiff of spicy pumpkin pie reminds you of a long-ago Thanksgiving dinner.

The smell of freshly washed sheets brings your cozy bed to mind.

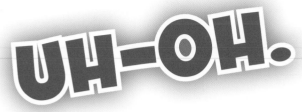

UH-OH.

I smell trouble. Sometimes things go wrong with your sense of smell.

Allergies or colds can block your nose with mucus. A head injury can damage the smelling parts of your brain. Some people are born with little ability to smell. And, many older people lose their ability to smell. If you cannot smell much at all, you have **anosmia**.

Take care of your nose—it's important! Never sniff housecleaning supplies or other things that might be harmful.

Have you ever noticed that some people are better smellers than others?

Some people's noses are super-sensitive. They are perfect for jobs in food or perfume factories. All day long, they sniff products to pick the best ones.

But even their noses can get tired. Dinner smells great when you first get home, doesn't it? But after a few breaths, you can't smell it any more. Your sensors need a rest. Try taking a break from setting the table. Go play outside to freshen up your nose!

Thanks for coming on this scent safari with me. I'd love to follow our noses even further.

We could dive in the sea to learn how fish smell in water. Smelling helps them find food and places to lay their eggs. Or we could travel from season to season. Can you smell more in warm or cold weather?

For now, keep your nose clean. Remember your sense of smell makes life happier and healthier. It's a truly scent-sational sense!

YOUR NOSE KNOWS

Everyone has a smell of his or her own. It's as special as a fingerprint. But do you know your parents' special smells? Try this test with a few friends.

Things you need:

shirt your mom has worn
shirt your dad has worn
blindfold or handkerchief

Ask your friends to bring shirts in plastic bags that their parents have worn for hours without washing. Then blindfold one friend. Can your friend pick out his or her parents' shirts by smell alone?

Give everyone a chance to try. Can anyone describe what he or she smells on the shirts?

GLOSSARY

anosmia (uh-NOZ-me-uh): If someone has anosmia, he or she lacks the sense of smell. Some people are born with anosmia.

germs (JURMS): Germs are tiny living things that can cause disease. The mucus in your nose stops germs from going into your body.

hippocampus (hip-uh-KAM-puss): The hippocampus is the part of the brain that forms, sorts, and stores memories. Smell messages go to the hippocampus.

mucus (MYOO-kuss): Mucus is a thick, sticky liquid that protects the nose, mouth, and throat. Mucus lines the inside of the nose.

nasal cavity (NAY-zul KAV-uh-tee): The nasal cavity is the space above the roof of the mouth. Smell sensors are found in the nasal cavity.

nerves (NURVS): Nerves are pathways that carry messages to or from the brain. Nerves carry messages about the things you smell.

odors (OH-durs): Odors are smells. Your smell sensors detect odors in the air.

olfactory bulb (ol-FAK-tu-ree BULB): The olfactory bulb is a part of the brain where smell sensors deliver messages. The olfactory bulb connects to smell sensors.

sense organs (SENSS OR-gins): Sense organs are body parts such as ears, eyes, nose, tongue, and skin that help you understand your world. The nose is one of your sense organs.

sensors (SEN-surs): Sensors are things that detect touch, heat, or smells. Some sensors in your body allow you to smell.

FURTHER READING

Cobb, Vicki. *Follow Your Nose: Discover Your Sense of Smell*. Brookfield, CT: Millbrook Press, 2000.

Collins, Andrew. *See, Hear, Smell, Taste, and Touch: Using Your Five Senses*. Washington DC: National Geographic, 2006.

Walker, Richard. *Eyewitness Human Body*. New York: DK Publishing, 2009.

Weiss, Ellen. *The Sense of Smell*. New York: Children's Press, 2009.

WEB SITES

Visit our Web site for links about your sensational sense of smell:

childsworld.com/links

Note to Parents, Teachers, and Librarians: We routinely verify our Web links to make sure they are safe and active sites. So encourage your readers to check them out!